飞向中文

Flying with Chinese

KA Student Book

© 2007 Marshall Cavendish International (Singapore) Private Limited

Published by Marshall Cavendish Education
A member of Times Publishing Limited
Times Centre, 1 New Industrial Road, Singapore 536196
Customer Service Hotline: (65) 6213 9106
E-mail: fps@sg.marshallcavendish.com
Website: www.marshallcavendish.com/education/sg

Distributed in North America by:

CHENG & TSUI COMPANY
Bringing Asia to the World™

Cheng & Tsui Company,
25 West St, Boston, MA 02111
www.cheng-tsui.com
Toll Free 1-800-554-1963

First published 2007

ISBN 978-981-01-6673-1

Publisher: Lim Geok Leng
Editors: Yvonne Lee Richard Soh Rita Teng Jo Chiu Hu Jingping Chong Liping
Chief Designer: Roy Foo

这是什么？

我会读 石

I can do these things in Chinese, can you?

I can...

❖ ask what something is

❖ ask for permission

❖ recognize the hanzi "石", know what it means and how to pronounce it

石头在哪里？

我会读 见

我会读 哪

我会读　谁

石头在哪里？

石　头，　　　石　头，

在 哪 里？　　在 哪 里？

石头你在哪里？ 石头你在 哪里？

不 见 了，　　　不 见 了！

山 八 川 小

I can do these things in Chinese, can you?

I can...

❖ ask where something is

❖ ask who someone is

❖ sing the song "石头在哪里"

❖ recognize the *hanzi* "小", know what it means and how to pronounce it

KA Workbook

© 2007 Marshall Cavendish International (Singapore) Private Limited

Published by Marshall Cavendish Education
A member of Times Publishing Limited
Times Centre, 1 New Industrial Road, Singapore 536196
Customer Service Hotline: (65) 6213 9106
E-mail: fps@sg.marshallcavendish.com
Website: www.marshallcavendish.com/education/sg

Distributed in North America by:

CHENG & TSUI COMPANY
Bringing Asia to the World™

Cheng & Tsui Company,
25 West St, Boston, MA 02111
www.cheng-tsui.com
Toll Free 1-800-554-1963

First published 2007

ISBN 978-981-01-6674-8

Publisher: Lim Geok Leng
Editors: Yvonne Lee   Richard Soh   Rita Teng   Jo Chiu   Hu Jingping   Chong Liping
Chief Designer: Roy Foo

第1课 这是什么？

妈妈，你看，这是什么？

啊，好奇怪的石头！

石头

 # 好奇怪的石头

石

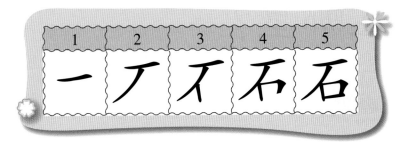

1	2	3	4	5
一	丆	石	石	石

I can do these things in Chinese, can you?

I can...

❖ ask what something is

❖ ask for permission

❖ recognize the *hanzi* "石", know what it means and how to pronounce it

	Date	Date

3

第2课 石头在哪里？

石头在哪里？

石头在……

小猴子，你是谁啊？

 小

1	2	3
丨	小	小

I can do these things in Chinese, can you?

I can...

❖ ask where something is

❖ ask who someone is

❖ sing the song "石头在哪里？" with the class

❖ recognize the hanzi "小", know what it means and how to pronounce it

	Date	Date

Flying with Chinese

KA Teacher Guide

© 2007 Marshall Cavendish International (Singapore) Private Limited

Published by Marshall Cavendish Education
A member of Times Publishing Limited
Times Centre, 1 New Industrial Road, Singapore 536196
Customer Service Hotline: (65) 6213 9106
E-mail: fps@sg.marshallcavendish.com
Website: www.marshallcavendish.com/education/sg

Distributed in North America by:

CHENG & TSUI COMPANY
Bringing Asia to the World™

Cheng & Tsui Company,
25 West St, Boston, MA 02111
www.cheng-tsui.com
Toll Free 1-800-554-1963

First published 2007

ISBN 978-981-01-6705-9

Publisher: Lim Geok Leng
Editors: Yvonne Lee   Richard Soh   Rita Teng   Jo Chiu   Hu Jingping   Chong Liping
Chief Designer: Roy Foo

Contents

CHAPTER 1 Introduction to *Flying with Chinese*

Children are natural language learners. Although Chinese may be considered very difficult by adults who do not speak it, children can learn it as naturally and joyfully as they learn any other language, including their own. This series is designed to make the most of the child's natural language learning ability, creating meaningful contexts for learning and guiding learners toward language proficiency and cultural appreciation. Each book is organized around a theme and integrated with other content areas in the elementary school curriculum.

The books and lessons in *Flying with Chinese* are standards based, designed thematically, and focused on student performance. These elements have guided the development of this program:

1. Thematic planning and instruction

2. "Standards for Chinese Language Learning," part of the *Standards for Foreign Language Learning in the 21st Century.*

3. Principles of *Understanding by Design*, 2nd Edition

4. Principles and structure of story form

5. Curriculum Development Framework for Language Learning

6. Making the match between languages and children (*Languages and Children: Making the Match*, 3rd Edition.)

THEMATIC PLANNING

Organizing units and lessons around a theme has a number of important benefits.

- It connects content, language, and culture to a "big idea," or enduring understanding, as recommended by *Understanding by Design*. (see discussion below)

- It makes instruction more understandable to learners, because the theme creates a meaningful context.

- It changes the instructional focus from *the language itself to the use of language* to achieve meaningful goals.

- It provides a rich context for standards-based learning. (see discussion below)

- It involves the students in real language use in a variety of situations, modes, and text types.

- It involves activities or tasks that can engage the learner in complex thinking and sophisticated use of language, even at early stages of instruction.

- It is brain-friendly, taking advantage of the brain's natural ability to make connections in the process of learning.

- It links language instruction to the philosophy and the content of the general elementary school curriculum.

STANDARDS AND CURRICULUM

The *Standards for Foreign Language Learning in the 21st Century*, of which the Chinese standards are a part, serves as a guide to what is important in the language classroom. They emphasize student performance, the actual use of language in meaningful ways.

The *Communication* standards remind us to give students experiences and assessments that focus on comprehension and presentation of information as well as on interaction. The *Cultures* and *Connections* standards call for the creation of rich contexts for language learning, drawn from the cultures being taught and from the general curriculum. The *Comparisons* standards encourage teachers to help students better understand their own language and culture as they begin to understand the new language and cultures. In the *Communities* standards teachers are reminded of the most important goals of language learning: real use of the new language beyond the classroom and development of a life-long interest and enthusiasm for language learning. Together the standards emphasize the importance of assessment of student performance.

For convenience in the planning of lessons, a summary of the standards is provided here. For further information, including Chinese language examples, see *Standards for Foreign Language Learning in the 21st Century*. 1999. Yonkers, NY: National Standards in Foreign Language Education Project. Ordering information can be found at www.actfl.org.

Communication: Goal One

Communicate in Chinese

Standard 1.1
Students engage in conversations, provide and obtain information, express feelings and emotions, and exchange opinions in Chinese.

Standard 1.2
Students understand and interpret written and spoken language on a variety of topics in Chinese.

Standard 1.3
Students present information, concepts, and ideas to an audience of listeners or readers on a variety of topics.

Cultures: Goal Two

Gain Knowledge and Understanding of the Cultures of the Chinese-Speaking World

Standard 2.1
Students demonstrate an understanding of the relationship between the practices and perspectives of the cultures of the Chinese-speaking world.

Standard 2.2
Students demonstrate an understanding of the relationship between the products and perspectives of the cultures of the Chinese-speaking world.

Connections: Goal Three

Connect with Other Disciplines and Acquire Information

Standard 3.1
Students reinforce and further their knowledge of other disciplines through the study of Chinese.

Standard 3.2
Students acquire information and recognize the distinctive viewpoints that are only available through the Chinese language and culture.

Comparisons: Goal Four

Develop Insight into the Nature of Language and Culture

Standard 4.1
Students demonstrate understanding of the nature of language through comparisons of the Chinese language with their own.

Standard 4.2
Students demonstrate understanding of the concept of culture through comparisons of Chinese culture with their own.

Communities: Goal Five

Participate in Multilingual Communities at Home and Around the World

Standard 5.1
Students use the Chinese language both within and beyond the school setting

Standard 5.2
Students show evidence of becoming life-long learners by using Chinese for personal enjoyment and enrichment.

The principles of backward planning/backward design, as developed in the popular book *Understanding by Design* (Wiggins and McTighe, 1998, 2005), guide the planning process for this program and for the language classroom. Like the Standards, backward design involves first deciding on the desired results of instruction, and then planning the content and the activities necessary to prepare student to achieve these results.

As a first step, the planner decides the enduring understandings, or "big ideas," that make this particular lesson or set of materials important enough to teach. An "enduring understanding (EU)" goes beyond the Chinese classroom to have lasting value in the lives and learning of the students. It is most clearly expressed in a sentence that begins, "Students will understand that…" For example, the EU for the first unit in this program is: Students will understand that they can use Chinese to make friends.

Once this EU has been identified, the actual goal of the unit is stated as an Essential Question (EQ). This question is usually stated in terms that a student would understand. For example, the EQ for the first unit in this program is: What do my new friends want to know about me? The EQ helps to clarify both the purpose and the goal of the unit.

The next step is to decide what evidence the teacher needs to be sure that students have successfully learned the material of the unit and gained the enduring understanding. This is usually expressed as one or more final products or performances (performance assessments), toward which the students are working throughout the unit. In this assessment the emphasis is on *performance*, actually demonstrating the new learning and understanding, and not just passing a test or telling what has been learned. In our standards-based curriculum, these performances include interpersonal, interpretive, and presentational communication. In addition to the final performance, or summative assessment, there will also be formative assessments along the way to help the teacher track the progress of individual students toward the unit goal.

In the *Flying with Chinese* program, the enduring understandings, essential questions, and performance assessments for each book guide the choice of all the materials and activities within the book, the workbook, and the Teacher's Guide. Together they serve as a kind of magnetic pole, defining "true North" for the textbook writers and for the Chinese teacher. When the Chinese teacher plans lessons and activities, she or he will use some of their own activities and resources in addition to the Teacher's Guide, the workbook, and the student book. These activities and resources can be chosen with confidence when they are always tested for their contribution to bringing students to the goal(s) described by the EU, the EQ, and the final assessment. The enduring understanding, essential questions, themes and sub-themes of this series are listed in the next chapter.

The steps in this backward design process are summarized here:

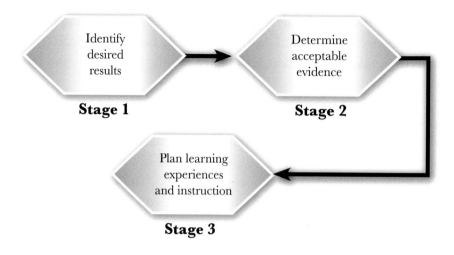

Stages in the Backward Design Process

Stage 1: Identify desired results
- What is worthy and requiring of understanding?
  ("Students will understand that...)

Stage 2: Determine acceptable evidence
- What is evidence of understanding?
  (Final product or performance)

Stage 3: Plan learning experiences and instruction
    (Always guided by "true North," the EU and the EQ)
- What learning experiences and teaching promote
  understanding, interest, excellence?

STORY FORM AND LESSON PLANNING

Story Form is a term developed by Kieran Egan, a Canadian researcher, and described in a number of his books, including Teaching As Storytelling: An Alternative Approach to Teaching and Curriculum in the Elementary School (1986). The authors of Flying with Chinese believe that good units, lessons, or activities all share the characteristics of a good story, including such elements as suspense, humor, surprises, and appeal to the emotions. Perhaps most important, there should be a clear-cut beginning, middle, and end, and the end point should provide students with a sense of completion, success, and pride. The most successful activities, lessons, and units should "land," in much the same way as a gymnast "sticks" a landing.

Story Form Structure

Beginning

• Motivation

• Engagement of the Learner

Middle

• Activity Toward a Goal

• Participation by the Learner

End

• Outcome • Product • Solution • Resolution

• Achievement of Goal by the Learner

In his "Story Form Framework" for primary school students (p.41), Egan suggests that planners always begin with these three questions, to determine what is most important in the material to be

Question from Story Form Framework	Example for the topic "family"
1. *What is most important about this topic?* (*for this unit or this lesson*)	Family members help and support each other in many different ways.
2. *Why should it matter to children?* (*or to learners*)	All children are part of some kind of family, and learning about other families helps them understand their own family situation.
3. *What is effectively engaging about it?*	The emotions associated with family relationships are among the deepest and the most basic, especially for children. "Helping" and "not helping" can be very emotional, especially among siblings

We encourage teachers to begin the planning of every lesson with these three questions, as we have tried to do in these Chinese materials.

The planning process for the teacher is very demanding, requiring numerous decisions at every step. Dahlberg has organized these teacher decisions in a graph that shows how all of the key decisions relate to one another (see below). Throughout the planning, every aspect of the unit and the lesson are brought together by the thematic center: Theme, Enduring Understandings/ Essential Questions, Standards, and Outcomes (Objectives).

Some of the resources for the planner, as recommended for the framework, include the following:
- *Standards*, local and state curriculum guides/frameworks
- Lists of language functions (language in use): see example below
- Culture Framework; symbols, products, practices
  (available for K-8 from Montgomery County Public Schools; 850 Hungerford Dr., Rockville, MD 20850 phone: 301-279-3911)
- Content guides for other curriculum areas
- ACTFL Student Performance Guidelines (See Appendix, *Languages and Children* or order from the ACTFL Web site: www.actfl.org)

In the books of the *Flying with Chinese* series, many of the themes have been based on stories chosen and developed to bring Chinese culture and history to life.

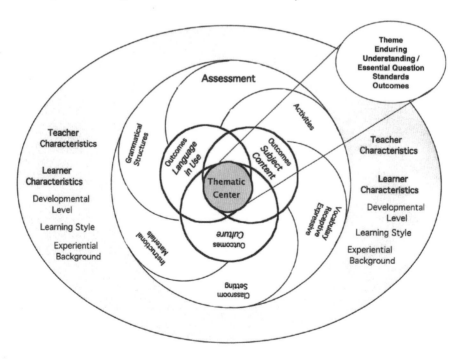

A Curriculum Development Framework for Language Learning 2005
Carol Ann Dahlberg • cadahlbe@cord.edu

Communicative Functions (Language Use)
Australian Language Levels Stages B – D (Middle Primary)

(both initiating and reacting)
Socializing
- using different modes of address
- inquiring about health
- greeting
- introducing
- thanking

Exchanging information
- identifying
- asking for/giving information describing
- narrating personal experiences
- inquiring about or expressing knowledge
- inquiring about or expressing opinions
- asking for/giving permission
- stating necessity and need
- inquiring about or expressing likes/dislikes/preferences
- inquiring about or expressing wishes

Getting things done
- requesting
- suggesting
- making arrangements
- reacting to offers, requests, suggestions, invitations
- inviting
- instructing

Expressing attitudes
- expressing admiration
- expressing approval/disapproval
- expressing interest/disinterest
- expressing friendship
- expressing regret
- expressing apology
- expressing need

Organizing and maintaining communication
- attracting attention
- expressing lack of comprehension
- asking for repetition or rephrasing
- asking how to say something in the target language
- asking how to spell something mentioned
- asking someone to explain what they just said

Australian Language Levels Guidelines, Book: Syllabus Development and Programming. Australia, Curriculum Development Centre.

GUIDING PRINCIPLES FOR *FLYING WITH CHINESE*

Teachers will have the greatest success with these materials if they follow these guidelines:

1. Teach 98-100 per cent of the time in Chinese.

2. Use Chinese for classroom management as well as for instruction.

3. Surround students with Chinese and give them extended listening experiences, through use of storytelling, story reading, Total Physical Response (TPR) activities, explanations, descriptions, and demonstrations. The language for these activities should be directed to the students' current comprehension level and slightly above (i+1)

4. Avoid translating from English to Chinese or from Chinese to English, and do not encourage students to translate. Clarify meaning through the use of visuals, gestures, physical activity, and clear context. Check for understanding using the same tools, and by asking students to perform with the new language.

5. Present vocabulary in functional chunks and in context, rather than as isolated words or lists.

6. Plan lessons that include a variety of activities, student groupings, and types of interaction that will appeal to differing learner interests and learning styles.

7. Use songs, rhymes, chants, and games to practice language and reinforce concepts.

8. Choose authentic songs, games, stories, and rhymes in preference to translations whenever possible.

9. Provide opportunities for learners to express personal meaning from the earliest stages of the program.

10. Encourage growing independence and independent language use on the part of learners, moving them toward increased expression of individual ideas and opinions.

REFERENCES AND RESOURCES

Australian Language Levels Guidelines, Book 2: Syllabus Development and Programming. Woden, A. C. T.: Curriculum Development Center, 1988, p. 69.

Curtain, Helena, and Carol Ann Dahlberg. *Languages and Children: Making the Match*. Third Edition New York: Pearson Publishing (Allyn & Bacon), 2004.

Egan, Kieran. Teaching as Storytelling: *An Alternative Approach to Teaching and Curriculum in the Elementary School*. Chicago: University of Chicago Press, 1986.

Standards for Foreign Language Learning in the 21st Century. Yonkers, NY: National Standards in Foreign Language Education Project, 1999.

Swender, Elvira, and Greg Duncan.. "ACTFL Performance Guidelines for K-12 Learners." *Foreign Language Annals* 31:4 (Winter, 1998):479-491.

Wiggins, Grant, and Jay McTighe. *Understanding by Design*. Expanded 2nd Edition. Alexandria, VA: ASCD, 2005.

CHAPTER 2

Overview of Language and Literacy Development in *Flying with Chinese*

HOW TO USE THIS PROGRAM

Flying with Chinese provides materials for kindergarten/pre-kindergarten through grade 6. The complete program consists 21 student books, each with an accompanying student workbook and a teacher guide. Each lesson in the student book and workbook is intended to provide materials for one week of classes that meet daily for 30 minutes. The teacher guide gives teachers the background for the program and general suggestions for planning and managing the Chinese classroom.

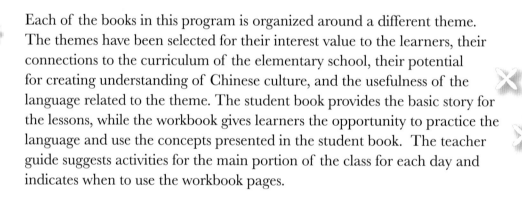

Each of the books in this program is organized around a different theme. The themes have been selected for their interest value to the learners, their connections to the curriculum of the elementary school, their potential for creating understanding of Chinese culture, and the usefulness of the language related to the theme. The student book provides the basic story for the lessons, while the workbook gives learners the opportunity to practice the language and use the concepts presented in the student book. The teacher guide suggests activities for the main portion of the class for each day and indicates when to use the workbook pages.

The overview of the books below summarizes the themes, oral language and literacy development for each of the books and provides a suggested layout from kindergarten through grade six. Programs that begin later than kindergarten, or that have more or less intensity than 30 minutes per day, can use the same materials over a longer or shorter period of time.

Flying with Chinese — Themes and Titles

Note:
Flying with Chinese is a series of 21 Student Books for 7 levels: Introductory Level and Grades 1-6. Accompanying the Student Books are Workbooks, Audio CDs and Teacher Guides.

	Introductory Level	Grade 1	Grade 2	Grade 3	Grade 4	Grade 5	Grade 6
Theme Focus	All About Me in My Chinese World	All About Families	My School Is a Community of Learning	I Am Important to My Community	I Can Explore My World Outdoors	I Am a Citizen of My Country	I Am Part of a Wide, Wide World
Theme A Everyone Is a Global Citizen	Just Imagine! An Introduction to Chinese — Sun Wukong Comes to Visit Me 孙悟空来看我	Families Help Each Other — My Uncle's Wedding 舅舅的婚礼	I Am Part of a School Community — A Big Performance 大表演	In a Community We Work Together — Happiness Is Helping People 助人为乐	What Can I Discover Beyond My Community? — Home 家	What Does It Mean to Be a Good Citizen? — Vote for Me 投我一票	Finding My Place in the Wide World — A Trip to China 中国游
including topics on • Geography • History • Civics							
Theme B Everyone Is Responsible for the Planet	My Body Connects Me to My World — My Friend Pingping 我的朋友平平	There Are All Kinds of Families — The Amazing Animal Race 动物大赛跑	I Can Discover How the World Works — Little Silk Worms, Big Discovery 小蚕茧, 大发现	I Live with Many Different Systems — Looking at Stars, Searching for Systems 看星星找系统	In What Ways Do Living Things Need Each Other? — Save the Panda! 保护熊猫	My Environment and I Influence Each Other — The Waste Detectives 环保侦探	Our Worlds Are Connected Through Time and Space — Our Ancient Modern World 古老的现代世界
including topics on • Science • Environment • Health • Mathematics							
Theme C Everyone Has a Cultural Heritage	Let Me Tell You Who I Am — My Birthday Party 我的生日会	A New Year's Visit to a Chinese Family — José's Chinese New Year 荷西的中国新年	Going to School with Chinese Friends — Letters from Mary 玛丽的信	Communities Work and Play Together — The Unforgettable Dragon Boat Festival 难忘的端午节	Finding China -- China Finds the World — Heroes of the Open Sea 航海探险家	What Is Culture? What Happens When People of Different Cultures Meet? — Travelers on the Silk Roads 丝路交流	Let's Go! --Going Places with Chinese — Flying with Chinese 飞向中文
including topics on • Arts • Music • Geography • History							

Distribution of Oral Language Profi

Introductory Level and Grades 1-6

	Introductory Level	Grade 1	Grade 2
Expected Oral Language Proficiency Level*	Junior Novice Low	Junior Novice Mid	Junior Novice Mid - High
***Pinyin* and Tones**	Tone Exercises	Tone Exercise in Combinations	Tone Exercise in Combinatio
***Hanzi* Acquisition**	30 *Hanzi*	30 New *Hanzi* (60 in total)	60 New *Hanzi* (120 in total)
	• Match *hanzi* that I have learned with pictures related to that *hanzi* • Find those *hanzi* that I have learned in posters, signs, or labels • Trace some *hanzi* on paper or in the air	• Match *hanzi* that I have learned with pictures related to that *hanzi* • Find those *hanzi* that I have learned in posters, signs, or labels • Say and write some *hanzi* that I have learned	• Match *hanzi* that I have learned with pictures rela to that *hanzi* • Find those *hanzi* that I ha learned in posters, signs, labels • Say and write some *hanz* that I have learned • Recognize words, phrases expressions written in *ha* • Copy what the teacher wr or from a sign, poster, or label
Sight Vocabulary Recognition	• Recognize some *hanzi* that we have read in the textbooks • Recognize a few *hanzi* in signs and/or labels in the classroom • Read some picture story books written in Chinese of similar reading levels, or read along when they are read to me	• Recognize some *hanzi* that we have read in the textbooks • Recognize some *hanzi* in signs and/or labels in the classroom • Read some picture story books written in Chinese of similar reading levels, or read along when they are read to me	• Recognize some *hanzi* that have read in the textbooks • Recognize some *hanzi* in s and labels in the classroom • Read some picture story books written in Chinese o similar reading levels, or re along when they are read t me

Note:
*Based on the Junior Proficiency Guidelines developed by the Center for Applied Linguistics (reference).   **ACTFL Performance Guidelines for K-12 Learners.

...ncy and Hanzi Literacy:

Grade 3	Grade 4	Grade 5	Grade 6
...Novice High – ...Intermediate Low	Junior Intermediate Low – Junior Intermediate Mid	Junior Intermediate Mid – Junior Intermediate High	Junior Intermediate High, or Intermediate Mid **
...uction of *Hanyu Pinyin*	Use *Pinyin* to Support the Learning and Using of *Hanzi*	Use *Pinyin* to Support the Learning and Using of *Hanzi*	Use *Pinyin* to Support the Learning and Using of *Hanzi*
...*Hanzi* (180 in total)	90 New *Hanzi* (270 in total)	100 New *Hanzi* (370 in total)	130 New *Hanzi* (500 in total)
<ul><li>...e *Hanyu pinyin* to ...nscribe Chinese sounds</li><li>...tch *hanzi* that I learned ...h pictures related to that ...nzi</li><li>...d those *hanzi* that I have ...rned in posters, signs, or ...els</li><li>...cognize words, phrases, or ...pressions written in *hanzi*</li><li>...py what the teacher writes ...from a sign, poster, or ...del</li><li>...e some *hanzi* that I have ...rned to write words, ...rases, or expressions that ...ll help me to communicate</li><li>...e a combination of *hanzi*, ...nyin, and/or pictures to ...rite, following a pattern ...format provided by the ...acher</li><li>...ead aloud what my friends ...d I have written</li></ul>	<ul><li>Use *Hanyu pinyin* to transcribe Chinese sounds</li><li>Find the *hanzi* that I have learned in posters, signs, or labels</li><li>Recognize words, phrases, or expressions written in *hanzi*</li><li>Use some *hanzi* that I have learned to write words, phrases, or expressions that will help me to communicate</li><li>Use a combination of *hanzi*, *pinyin*, and/or pictures to write, following a pattern or format provided by the teacher</li><li>Read aloud what my friends and I have written</li></ul>	<ul><li>Use *pinyin* to input *hanzi* on a computer for communication</li><li>Understand words, phrases, or expressions that contain *hanzi* I have learned</li><li>Use *hanzi* I have learned to write words, phrases, expressions, short notes or messages for communication</li><li>Use a combination of *hanzi* and/or *pinyin*, with the aid of a dictionary, to write, following a pattern or format provided by the teacher</li><li>Read aloud what my friends and I have written</li></ul>	<ul><li>Use *pinyin* to input *hanzi* on a computer for communication</li><li>Understand words, phrases, or expressions that contain *hanzi* I have learned</li><li>Use *hanzi* I have learned to write words, phrases, expressions, notes or short passages for communication</li><li>Use *pinyin* and a dictionary as tools to engage in extended pieces of writing in *hanzi*, following a pattern or format provided by the teacher</li><li>Read aloud what my friends and I have written</li></ul>
<ul><li>...ad the textbook with the ...lp of the teacher or another ...inese-speaking adult</li><li>...cognize some signs and ...els in the classroom or ...blic places</li><li>...ad some picture story ...oks written in Chinese of ...milar reading levels, or read ...ong when they are read to ...e</li></ul>	<ul><li>Read the textbook with the help of the teacher or another Chinese-speaking adult, or with *pinyin* transcription</li><li>Recognize some *hanzi* in signs and/or labels in the classroom or public places</li><li>Read some books or other materials written in Chinese of similar reading levels, or read along when they are read to me</li></ul>	<ul><li>Read the textbook with the help of the teacher or another Chinese-speaking person, or with *pinyin* transcription</li><li>Read some signs and/or labels written in *hanzi* in the classroom or public places</li><li>Read some books or other materials written in Chinese of similar reading levels, or read along when they are read to me</li></ul>	<ul><li>Read the textbook with the help of the teacher or another Chinese-speaking person, or with *pinyin* transcription</li><li>Read some signs and/or labels written in *hanzi* in the classroom or public places</li><li>Read some books or other materials written in Chinese of similar reading levels, or read along when they are read to me</li></ul>

CHAPTER 3

Instructional and Assessment Strategies

SOME BASIC UNDERSTANDINGS

How children learn languages: a few principles

Language development for young learners takes place in predictable stages, as described by second language acquisition research. The first stage of language learning takes place primarily through listening. Learners use all available clues to gain meaning from the language they hear and see around them—gestures, facial expressions, body language, visuals, and context.

At first they listen primarily for meaning, i.e., what does someone want me to do, what is the story about? Teachers can use many strategies to give students a rich language environment during these early stages. One of the most effective is a "thinking aloud" strategy, in which teachers talk about what they are doing as they are doing it, being careful to use language with a lot of repetition that students will be able to understand.

For example:
"Now I will pass out the crayons. Mary, here is a red crayon for you. I'll lay this crayon beside your pencil. Here is a green crayon for you, Jose. I'll lay this crayon on top of your paper." And so on. Or, "I want to show you a picture. Let's see, where did I put that picture? Is it on top of my desk? No, where did I put it? Is it in my briefcase? Yes, here it is."

To help students understand and begin to feel comfortable with their new language, teachers use a number of techniques for making their message clear. The teacher should use natural language, but with certain adaptations:

1. A somewhat slower rate of speech (still within normal rate of speech for that speaker, but at the slower end of the range—not distorted)

2. More distinct pronunciation (not distorted pronunciation, however, which actually changes the sounds of the language)

3. Shorter, less complex sentences

4. More rephrasing and repetition

5. More frequent meaning checks with the listener to make sure she or he is understanding

6. Use of gestures and visual reinforcement

7. Greater use of concrete objects, pictures, and acting out of meanings

(adapted from *Languages and Children*, pp. 2-3)

It is natural for beginning learners to spend time just listening and understanding, without trying to say anything in the language. This is known as the *silent period*, and it may last for a longer or shorter period of time depending on the individual learner. During the silent period, learners are developing a bank of meanings associated with the new language.

Once learners have the motivation, the confidence, and the opportunity to communicate something in the new language, they draw on their stored bank of meanings and language to construct a message. When they begin to speak, they also begin to listen in a new way. Instead of listening only for meaning, they now listen also for how the new language is put together. For this reason it continues to be important to surround students with language after they have begun to speak.

Teaching in the Target Language

The books and lessons in *Flying with Chinese* are designed for classrooms in which Chinese is the language of instruction 95-100 percent of the time. It is intended that all instruction and classroom management should be conducted in Chinese, and that translation to or from the students' native language should happen rarely, if at all. At the same time, students should not be asked to demonstrate their understanding by giving the meaning of a word or phrase in their native language, nor allowed to shout out meanings in their native language to help one another.

Teaching in the target language has a number of advantages for the Chinese language classroom.

- Learners need to be surrounded with language that they understand and that is meaningful to them, as a first step in language learning. This type of language is called *comprehensible input* (Krashen, 1973). A classroom that functions consistently in Chinese gives learners the best possible environment for second language acquisition.

- Students need *opportunity* and reasons to use the language. When the classroom functions in Chinese, there is much greater motivation for students to learn and use Chinese in order to get what they want and need. When students know that they will need to use Chinese themselves, they will begin to listen to the language of their teacher in a new way, in preparation for communicating something themselves.

- Target language instruction is *brain compatible* instruction. The brain is especially skilled at discovering patterns and making meanings. When learners are surrounded with meaningful language in rich contexts, the brain has the best conditions for doing what it does best.

- The target language is the key or "ticket" to the *target culture*. When students are functioning in a target-language environment, they are preparing for a time when they can actually enter that culture and participate in it.

While there are situations when the native language must be used, we recommend keeping these at a minimum, and keeping a clear separation between Chinese and the native language. It is helpful to have a visual signal to indicate when Chinese is the language of the classroom and when it is permissible to speak the native language (see description later in this introduction). It is both distracting and counter-productive to move back and forth between Chinese and the native language, and in most cases translation will encourage students to rely on their native language rather than taking the risk of *Flying with Chinese*.

USEFUL STRATEGIES THAT EMPHASIZE LISTENING

Meaningful listening experiences are essential for language learners at beginning stages, and they continue to be important after students begin speaking. Listening experiences often serve as the foundation for later speaking, reading, and writing activities.

Total Physical Response (TPR)

One of the most useful strategies for early language learning is Total Physical Response (TPR) developed by James Asher and popularized by many workshop leaders and teachers. TPR is a good way to connect language to meaning through actions, and without translation. These basic steps can be used to introduce new vocabulary through TPR:

Steps	Examples
1. *Give a command while modeling the action.* a. start with actions using the body b. give commands involving objects c. use commands relating to pictures, maps, and charts, etc.	a. "Raise your hand." "Turn around." "Put your hand on your knee." b. "Pick up your book and lay it under your chair." c. "Go to the map and point to China." "Go to the (picture of the) bathroom and brush your teeth."
2. *After several repetitions of the command, remove the teacher model. If students can respond without the model, give the command a few more times. Mix up single commands and give them in a different order.*	"Put your hand on your knee." "Turn around." "Raise your hand."
3. *After students respond confidently to a number of single commands, combine them in original and **unexpected** ways. Surprise and humor are key elements of TPR.*	"Put your hand on your _____ knee." (new combinati_____
4. *Call on volunteers to respond to commands of increasing length and complexity (often silly), **using familiar language in new combinations.***	"Who can do _____ to the map _____ and put _____ Maria _____

5. *String commands together to tell a story or create a sequence that has a beginning, middle, and end.*	"Mary, put your left hand on the panda's head. Mario, put your right elbow on the panda's foot. Liming, put your elbow on the panda's nose. (and so on) Class, take out your (imaginary) cameras and take a picture. Smile!!"
6. *Give student volunteers the opportunity to give commands to the rest of the class (role reversal).*	"Who would like to be laoshi today?"
7. *Extend oral TPR activities into experiences with reading and/or writing.*	"What was the funniest command Mario gave you? Let's write it down on the white board." "Who can do the activity we wrote one the white board yesterday?"

In addition to using TPR to introduce new language in a playful manner, the teacher can also use TPR techniques whenever giving directions for an activity or introducing new directions for classroom management. In TPR, commands are never translated, and vocabulary is not pre-taught. Students learn to understand by imitating teacher actions and they remember because of the physical involvement. As learners respond to new combinations of vocabulary in familiar commands, they grow in confidence that they can construct meaning in the new language.

Because TPR gives learners the opportunity to receive, process, and store linguistic input for an extended period time, they are able to "notice" the presence of a specific feature in the input and/or comprehend the meaning of the feature. This ability to notice will eventually enable learners to transfer the training in listening to other skills—speaking, reading and writing—and will encourage them to continue studying the target language and to display more positive attitudes (For further information, see Asher, 2000, Ellis, 1994).

Gouin Series

This strategy is another combination of language and actions. It differs from TPR in several ways. While TPR is most successful when there are strong components of surprise and the unexpected, the Gouin series consists of an unvarying sequence of actions, with a clear-cut beginning, middle and end. It was developed by 19th-century French linguist François Gouin, and adapted for modern classrooms by Dr. Constance Knop (University of Wisconsin-Madison).

series can be used to introduce a series of actions within a specific context, or it can story in the lesson. It is a flexible tool that can be used for many different purposes. The example below could be used to teach appropriate behavior when a student wishes to go to the bathroom.

Gouin Series Components	Example
• introduction to set the scene and motivate the action • 6-8 statements (can also use commands) • 7-syllable limit for most statements • logical sequence of actions • single, specific, clear context • action verbs • one tense (not necessarily present) • one person (not necessarily first person singular) • simple props or visuals to dramatize the action	Teacher (shows dirty hands) says, "Ooh, my hands are dirty." I raise my hand. I say, "May I please go to the bathroom?" I stand up. I take the pass. I walk to the bathroom. I wash my hands. I go back to the classroom. I lay the pass down. I sit down.

1. Teacher presents series orally, accompanying words with pantomime, props.

2. Teacher repeats series orally and class joins in with pantomime, *not with words*.

3. Class pantomimes the series as teacher repeats orally but does not model actions. When moving to this step, the teacher first repeats the phrase and hesitates, to see if the students perform the pantomime on their own. If they cannot, the teacher models the action again. Continue this once or twice, until the students can perform the pantomime confidently.

4. Teacher makes a "mistake" in the sequence, perhaps leaving something out, to see if students catch it and correct the teacher.

5. Individual *volunteers* pantomime the series as teacher repeats orally, without modeling. Do until everyone has had a chance to "solo." With very confident students, teacher can "make mistakes," as with the whole group, to test for listening comprehension.

6. Class imitates series orally as well as physically, first together and then as individual volunteers leading the class.

Literacy transition (optional)

7. Teacher distributes cards with the steps of the series written on them, holding each card up and having the class repeat the phrase as they "read" the card.

8. Class and teacher repeat the series, and students hold up the correct card as their phrase is recited and then stand in front of the room in the order of the series.

9. Whole class "reads" the series from the cards in the front of the room.

10. Teacher distributes sheets of paper on which the steps of the series are written in the correct order, with a picture frame above each step. Students illustrate the "story" and

USEFUL STRATEGIES FOR MOVING FROM LISTENING TO SPEAKING: BUILDING FUNCTIONAL CHUNKS

Meaningful listening experiences are essential for language learners at beginning stages, and they Even during an early "silent period" of second language acquisition, we can give students toe-holds in spoken Chinese. In TPR and the Gouin series above, students are moved naturally into speaking, sometimes individually and sometimes with the group. Teachers can help students begin to use Chinese meaningfully if they are conscious of teaching "functional chunks" of language, memorized phrases that will help students to communicate meaningfully. These are some ways to teach these functional chunks.

Passwords and Language Ladders

There are certain phrases that are necessary for students to use in order to keep the classroom in the Chinese language. These phrases can be taught one at a time as *Passwords and Language Ladders*, and posted in the classroom with pictures that indicate their meaning. *Passwords* are usually chosen from those phrases that students repeatedly try to use in their native language, such as "Would you repeat that, please?" or "May I go to the bathroom?" On the day the are taught, students may be required to say the *Passwords* before leaving the classroom for recess or for their next class. As an alternative, the teacher may have all the children standing and let each child sit down after saying the *Passwords*. Once a *Passwords* has been taught and posted in the classroom, students are expected to use the Chinese phrase whenever they need it. If they try to use their native language, the teacher points to the password and prompts the appropriate Chinese phrase.

Language Ladders are similar to *Passwords* except that they are usually different ways of expressing the same idea. For example, a set of English phrases for a language ladder might be various ways of praising a person during group work: "Good job! Good work! That's a good idea! That's a good point!" The phrases for a language ladder are taught one at a time and then hung from cords or on a chain to show their relationship.

For more information about *Passwords* and *Language Ladders*, see *Languages and Children*, p. 49-51. A suggested list of Chinese passwords is found at the end of the Introduction.

Games

Games, especially culturally authentic games, are ideal for encouraging students to speak and for giving them practice with functional chunks of language. It is important to choose (or invent) games in which using Chinese is an essential element of the game. The game should require chunks of language, rather than just single words. In a favorite guessing game, for example, one child leaves the room and the teacher gives an object (perhaps a rock, from Book 1), to one of the children in the game circle, who hides the rock behind the back. The children all call (for example), "Mary, Mary, come back in. Come and find the rock." Mary comes back in and asks each child in turn, "Have you seen my rock?" The child responds, "No, I haven't seen it." The child holding the rock brings it out, when asked, and says, "Yes, I have your rock." Mary chooses another child to go out, and the game continues.

Rhymes, Chants, and Songs

Children love rhythm, rhymes, and songs. Both rhymes and songs can be chosen from the Chinese culture or created by the teacher to a familiar melody. They should be chosen to give children practice with meaningful, functional chunks of language, as well as for their cultural or thematic content. In addition, any chunk of language that a teacher wants children to practice can be turned into a chant and performed while marching, walking around the room, clapping, or making transitions from one activity to another. For example, children might chant "I want to play ball with you," in book 1. The combination of rhythm and movement helps children to remember the language, and the fun of the activity makes them want to say it again and again.

Partner Activities

Even very young children can do activities with a partner, and a number of simple partner activities will be described in the teacher guides for individual books. One simple activity, however, can be used over and over and every day to help learners become confident with important functional chunks of language. After introducing a phrase for children to practice, the teacher says, "Turn to your partner and…" For example, after introducing the phrase "Good morning," the teacher says, "Turn to your partner and tell your partner 'good morning.'" After deciding as a class that the weather for the day is sunny, the teacher says, "Turn to your partner and tell your partner, 'It's sunny today.'" After the group sings a new song, the teacher says, "Tell your partner 'You sing very well.'"

When the teacher does this simple partner exchange frequently, learners feel less self-conscious about speaking the language, and they practice in an enjoyable and non-threatening way. They may also begin to rely less on the teacher and more on one another.

NATURAL APPROACH QUESTIONING SEQUENCE

The Natural Approach is a methodology developed by Stephen Krashen and Tracy Terrell (1983), based on research in second language acquisition. It emphasizes the importance of an active listening phase, as mentioned above, and suggests specific strategies for developing skills in speaking, reading, and writing. Natural Approach suggests a useful sequencing of teacher questions to help move students from listening to speaking:

Natural Approach Steps	Examples
Step 1: Student responds with a name	Who has a red shirt? 谁有红衬衫? Who is holding the rock? 谁拿着石头?
Step 2: Yes-no question	Is Chen Lin wearing a red shirt? 陈铃穿着红衬衫吗? Is Betty holding the rock? 贝蒂拿着石头吗?
Step 3: Either-or questions, using nouns, verbs, adjectives, adverbs, or actions	Is Chen Lin wearing a red shirt or a blue shirt? 陈铃穿着红衬衫还是蓝衬衫? Is Betty holding the rock or the flower? 贝蒂拿着石头还是花? Is the rock big or small? 石头大还是小? Does the monkey feel happy or sad? 猴子快乐还是难过?
Step 4: What, when, where, who questions (Students answer with a single word, moving toward a phrase answer.)	What is Chen Lin wearing? 陈铃穿着什么? What is Betty holding? 贝蒂拿着什么?
Step 5: Students answer with the entire sentence or action.	What kind of rock is this? 这是什么样的石头? How does the monkey feel? 猴子觉得怎么样? What is Betty doing? 贝蒂在做什么? Tell us about this rock. 跟我们说一说这个石头有什么特别。

Teachers may find it useful to plan their questioning around this sequence of questions, moving from the easiest (Step 1) to the most difficult (Step 5). Note that there is a big jump from Step 3 to Step 4, where the answer is no longer embedded in the question. If a student has trouble answering a question at Step 4, for example, the teacher can rephrase the question to make it a Step 3 question, and so on. Using these strategies, the teacher can help students to have success experiences as they begin to speak Chinese.

IMPORTANT CONCEPTS AND USEFUL STRATEGIES FOR BUILDING READING AND WRITING UPON ORAL PROFICIENCY

Literacy development is built upon a solid foundation of oral proficiency. Teachers of young learners should also pay attention to their developmental readiness such as motor skills and cognitive maturity. On the other hand, students must be exposed to Chinese characters (called hanzi in this series) as early as possible and become familiar with important concepts and components of hanzi. Generally speaking, the guiding principle of this series is captured in the following question: Is this hanzi essential for students to know in this grade?

The *Flying with Chinese* program is based on the belief that students should begin with understanding the form of hanzi; i.e., that Chinese characters are two dimensional in square form (方块字). This is very different from alphabets that are uni-dimensional. Young learners also need to know that hanzi are not lines or strokes randomly put together. There are components that indicate sounds or meaning, and which must be written in certain order. If they use strategies, they will be able to memorize hanzi effectively, instead of trying to memorize all of them one by one.

In Grades K-2, students are introduced to isolated hanzi, with emphasis on tracing, copying, and recognition of sound, meaning, and form. In Grade 3 and beyond, students need to know how to combine individual hanzi into meaningful words, phrases, expressions, and sentences in context.

Teachers must differentiate the rate of oral proficiency and literacy acquisition. That is, literacy should be built upon the foundation of oral proficiency. This also means that students may need to know how to say something in Chinese, but not necessarily need to know how to write it. There is a distinction between *writing hanzi* and *using hanzi* to write. It is also recommended that the keyboard and computer be used as early as possible. In this instance, recognition of the right hanzi to choose from the word bank provided by computer software is even more critical. The ability to recognize and use the correct hanzi to write on a computer will enhance students' writing skills exponentially.

One strategy for building literacy upon oral proficiency is to use the Hanyu Pinyin pronunciation system that uses alphabets to indicate sounds of hanzi. Mastery of Hanyu Pinyin is also critical for students using Chinese word processing on the computer. In consideration of the fact that young learners are simultaneously learning English alphabets and phonics, the teaching and learning of Hanyu Pinyin is not introduced until Grade 3. By this time, students already have a solid foundation in English phonics, which could also serve as the foundation for Chinese phonology that combines consonants and vowels, or initials or finals as they are called in Hanyu Pinyin.

Some useful strategies for developing literacy in Chinese include:

- Write in the air （空中写字）
- Trace (描红)
- Hand copy
- Bingo
- Flash cards
- Card games
- Identification of hanzi in labels, signs, flyers, posters or passages
- Classification by radicals, sounds, or meaning
- Matching

More detailed strategies are listed in the Teacher's Guide of each book.

THE ROLE OF GRAMMAR

The structures and functions of the Chinese language are embedded in the student books and workbooks of this series, and they are practiced in context. Young children learn grammar primarily "through the ears," so grammar instruction is focused on usage rather than on rules. Teachers can help their students to develop good, grammatical language habits by choosing and inventing enjoyable songs, games, and chants that provide practice with grammatical structures while also supporting the theme of the lesson. The task of the entire PK to Grade 6 curriculum is to develop a language base for the learners that can later (in middle school and above) be analyzed and organized into a grammatical framework.

When children ask questions about the grammar of the new language, or notice similarities and differences in comparison with their native language, the teacher can offer a brief explanation without presenting an entire grammatical lecture. The teacher can make corrections based on usage, rather than citing a grammatical rule. If further discussion is desired, the teacher and students together might think of additional instances of the same usage, and even practice them together.

Although PK-6 language teachers do not systematically teach grammar, they are systematic and intentional about presenting materials and activities that help learners to become effective users of the grammar of Chinese. In the early books of this series, the grammar is located primarily in the "I can" statement.

PERFORMANCE-BASED ASSESSMENT

Each of the books in *Flying with Chinese* is designed to culminate in a performance assessment that gives students the opportunity to use the new language they have learned and combine it with previous learning. The goals of the entire book and workbook are guided by this final assessment. There are also assessments suggested for individual lessons, to help teachers monitor the performance of all the children in the class. We have provided sample rubrics for student performances in the appendix for the Teacher's Guide.

We recommend that teachers monitor and record student performance regularly, so that students who are lagging behind can be identified promptly and receive special attention. One effective strategy for regular student monitoring is to identify five students each day for special notice, and then to record their performance at the end of the class period on a checklist. Be sure that an individual student is not always monitored on the same day of the week—sometimes Fridays or Mondays can be "down" days for the whole class, for example.

I Can Statements

At the end of each lesson there is a section that contains several *I can* statements. These statements serve several purposes. First, they serve as a review that summarizes the important ideas or language skills that students need to know and be able to demonstrate. For this age group, the contextualized *I can* statements work more effectively than other kinds of review. Second and more important, they are reminders of the big ideas that help teachers to prioritize and focus their instruction. Frequently teachers lose sight of where they are going, or become too ambitious in trying to teach students too many ideas, concepts or skills. These statements serve as guideposts by which teachers can assess learning.

Generally speaking, because of the age of this group, teachers can either ask the class as a whole to respond to the questions, or a teacher or aide can ask students these questions individually. Because these assessment statements are in performance terms, students usually need to demonstrate what they can do besides making a check mark next to the statement.

REFERENCES AND RESOURCES

- Asher, James. *Learning Another Language through Actions*. 6th edition. Sky Oaks, California: Sky Oaks Productions, 2000.

- Ellis, Rod. *The Study of Second Language Acquisition*. Oxford: Oxford University Press, 1994.

- Krashen, Stephen D., and Tracy Terrell. *The Natural Approach. Language Acquisition in the Classroom*. San Francisco, CA: Alemany Press, 1983

- Krashen, S. (1973). Lateralization, language learning and the critical period: some new evidence. *Language Learning, 23*. pp. 63-74.

CHAPTER 4

Flying with Chinese from Day to Day

GOALS OF THIS BOOK

Our goals for the language development of students in kindergarten group are listed in the table below. Language Proficiency descriptions are based on the SOPA and ELLOPA levels published by the Center for Applied Linguistics (www.cal.org):

Language Proficiency Expectation	Expectations Related to Pronunciation	Expectations for Literacy Development
Junior Novice Low *Comprehension*: Students recognize isolated words and high frequency expressions taught in class. *Functional Ability*: Students produce isolated words and/or high frequency expressions taught in class; they have little functional communicative ability. *Vocabulary*: recognize and use words and expressions related to concrete objects and actions on learned topics. *Grammar*: use memorized chunks accurately, but lack grammar awareness. For this age group, grammar and language functions are expressed in terms of I can statements.	Students are able to imitate Laoshis to produce Chinese sounds in correct tones. The vocabulary glossary at the end of the Student Book provides *hanyu pinyin*, but students are not introduced to the *Hanyu Pinyin* pronunciation system.	Through the Student Book that is written in hanzi only, students develop emerging literacy. Students are expected to recognize ten basic pictographs that are introduced, and identify their meanings and pronunciation. Through the practice writing of these hanzi, students understand that strokes are meaningful components of hanzi, which should be written in a certain way following a certain order. Although reproduction of hanzi is not required at this level, students' "writing" will approximate that of real hanzi. They are encouraged to develop sight vocabulary of the text, signs and labels in the classroom.

These descriptions provide a generic learner profile for this age group. The overarching linguistic, content-related, cultural, and literacy objectives for each volume are stated at the beginning of each set of lesson plans for each volume, and the specifics are further explained under related units in each book.

Language Use in the Classroom

As discussed in the framework, we recommend the use of Chinese exclusively in class, supported by gestures, concrete objects, and many different visual or nonverbal cues. For those (infrequent) occasions when English must be used, we suggest that the Laoshi use a fan with the picture of a familiar US icon that all students can recognize; e.g., Mickey Mouse. When students see the picture of this icon, they will know that English is the language of the classroom. Once the Laoshi is finished with the use of English, the fan is turned to the other side with a Panda's or another familiar Chinese cultural icon's face, indicating the use of Chinese from that time on.

In this Guide, we provide you with a picture of a panda as the Chinese icon. Copyright restrictions prevent us from providing a picture of most familiar American popular icons, but they are usually available in clip-art form on the internet. If you want to use a picture of Mickey Mouse, for example, you may go online at www.mickey-mouse.com/themouse.htm, or find other pages using a search engine.

Emphasis on Listening:
The Use of TPR (Total Physical Response) and other Activities that Emphasize Listening

It is one of the important principles of this program to use only Chinese in the classroom, at least 95-100 percent of the time. Especially with the youngest students, much of the spoken Chinese will come from the Laoshi. Students will respond by following directions and participating in many non-verbal ways, including gestures and body language.

In this volume we often suggest the use of TPR (Total Physical Response) methodology (Asher, 1977). Although TPR can be used at all levels of language instruction, it is often used at the beginning level in which learners are offered extensive opportunities to listen. Instead of being required to produce the target language, learners are asked to respond to oral commands by carrying out the actions according to their understanding. TPR is frequently used to teach lexical items or carefully planned grammatical structures. For a detailed guidelines for conducting TPR activities, see the general introduction.

Research has provided evidence for the usefulness of TPR in developing learners' listening comprehension and vocabulary. It has been shown to help learners to rely less on translation and to listen for meaning. It also helps learners to develop better understanding of new materials while building short-term and long-term memory. In this age group, the use of TPR is similar to first language learning, in that young children focus on meaning rather than worrying about the form of the language.

Another frequent strategy is "Pingping says," a variation on the popular "Simon says" game, in which children follow commands only when they are preceded by the phrase "Simon says." For young children, there is just as much play value without requiring the phrase "Pingping says"; they simply enjoy doing what the leader tells them to. There is also an advantage for the Laoshi in this variation, because the Laoshi is better able to determine which children have understood the language. As children become more confident with the language, they may volunteer to be Pingping and lead the activity.

Throughout this series, we frequently refer to the use of TPR. In a few cases TPR is being used as a generic term for a listening activity that requires learners to show some kind of response. It is important for Laoshis to provide rich linguistic input through various types of activities and media, including TPR, story telling, audio- or video tapes, CDs, DVDs, and other guest or native speakers. While Laoshis may want to elicit some speech in Chinese from children, it is important to keep in mind that children should be asked to **act out** before they can **speak out**. Similarly, in assessing children's achievement in the Chinese language, Laoshis need to take into account what children are able to demonstrate through their actions, in addition to monitoring their Chinese language production.

Use of Story Telling

All children love stories. Every class should include at least one story, long or short, because stories help children to remember the new language as a whole, instead of struggling with isolated pieces of vocabulary. Laoshis can read stories from "big books," or from other picture books, in which pictures help to establish meaning for the listeners. The Laoshi may make up a story to connect new vocabulary in interesting and sometimes humorous ways. Children can help to create "new" stories by changing one or two characters in a story they know well.

Stories are especially effective if children can participate in them with actions and pantomime. TPR commands can be organized to create a story, with a beginning, middle, and end. Young children should never be expected to sit still without being involved, both mentally and physically—but stories have an amazing power to engage the learner and sustain attention.

As mentioned in the general introduction, every activity can be more engaging and more effective if it has the qualities of a good story.

Tone Exercise

Although the differentiation of tones in Mandarin is not introduced formally at this level, it is important to bring students' attention to tones. Laoshis are strongly advised to spend two minutes or so during each period to practice tones beginning with the second volume of the series. Through game-like activities, such as Copy Cat, Laoshis say sounds with the designated tones and demonstrate the arm position for the tone(s) being practiced. Students, like copy cats, imitate the Laoshi.

Literacy Practice

As part of Chinese cultural practice in communicating about hanzi, just as English speakers spell out letters for each other to indicate how to write a certain word, Chinese people often write in the air to indicate which hanzi is being referred to. As a way to develop literacy, Chinese children of this age group are taught, by waving their arms in the air, to imitate the Laoshi. There are a variety of ways of doing this, which are suggested below:

- Ask students to raise their arms to imitate the Laoshi to trace or write hanzi in the air. Laoshi can use a puppet/stuffed animal to lead the class to practice.

- Ask students to use their head, body, or foot to write hanzi in the air.

- Students can also practice by "writing" with their finger in a mini sand box or rice box, or by using water or a marker to write on the board.

- When students show evidence of acquiring hanzi, they can be the commander and ask other students or a stuffed animal to write.

For the Kindergarten and First grade students, writing hanzi is not required. Students are only expected to trace and recognize the hanzi taught, i.e., to know how to pronounce and connect meaning to sound and form. Those students who demonstrate more advanced motor skills and cognitive ability are of course allowed to read and write hanzi as they make progress. Having said that, we strongly encourage Laoshis to decorate their classrooms with as many posters, pictures, icons, art work, and authentic artifacts or realia as possible. These materials will create a culturally and linguistically rich environment for the students.

We also recommend that Laoshis stock as many Chinese children's books in the classrooms as possible, particularly big books. As each hanzi is being introduced, Laoshis can ask students to identify the specific hanzi being studied on posters, signs, or book covers. These resources will also be useful in the development of interpretive and presentational communication.

Variation in Class Activities

In any good language classrooms, particularly those for young learners, instruction must be differentiated according to the abilities and interests of learners. All children need opportunities to listen, speak, read, write, explore, and play with the language. With very young children, variety and movement are essential components of every class. New activities can be introduced during circle time, with children and Laoshi sitting in a circle on the floor. This brings children face-to-face with the Laoshi and all their classmates. This time should be alternated with table time—activities that require writing in a workbook, or doing a Chinese craft, for example—and with activities that require moving around the room. In classes that are longer than 30 minutes each day, the Laoshi may wish to develop centers for small-group work, i.e., a listening center, a game center, a writing center, among others. This kind of variation will help to meet the needs and interests of each student.

As a rough gauge for the length of activities, we suggest that activities last about the same number of minutes as the age (in years) of the children in the class. Activities should vary between those that require listening and concentration and those that allow for more movement on the part of the children.

Formative assessment: *I can* statements

At the end of each lesson, there is a section that contains several *I can* statements. These statements serve several purposes. First, they are like a review that summarizes the important ideas or language skills that students need to know and be able to demonstrate. For this age group, the contextualized *I can* statements work more effectively than grammatical review. Second and more important, they are reminders of the big ideas that help Laoshis to prioritize and focus their instruction. In trying to provide children with a rich language learning environment, Laoshis may lose sight of where they are going, or become overly ambitious in expecting students to master too many ideas, concepts or skills. These statements serve as guideposts by which Laoshis can assess learning.

Generally speaking, because of the age of this group, Laoshis can either ask the class as a whole to respond to the questions, or Laoshi or an aide can ask students these questions individually. Because these assessment statements are in performance terms, students usually need to demonstrate what they can do besides making a check mark next to the statement.

Culminating Performance Tasks

The final lessons in the book prepare the students to transfer the understandings and skills they have learned to a different, though similar, context. These culminating tasks give the student a sense of accomplishment and help the teacher to gauge the effectiveness of student learning. The performance tasks are opportunities for students to demonstrate the knowledge and skills in the "I can" statements.

HOW TO USE THE STUDENT BOOK AND WORKBOOK

The student book and workbook are interrelated in a complementary fashion. The former introduces the language and concepts, while the latter reinforces them. The workbook can be used as material for classroom activity or preparation for assessment. It can also function as homework to be applied in family and community situations. As emphasized throughout the entire series of *Flying with Chinese*, classroom activities, learning, instruction, and application of the Chinese language and culture are not limited to paper and pencil. Particularly suited for young learners is the notion of listening for an extended period of time and natural language use in real life situations. Therefore, the use of student and work books must be embedded in a rich context of games, songs, rhymes, and other interactive activities.

CLASSROOM MANAGEMENT

Rules

From the very beginning, it is wise to establish rules and expectations for classroom behavior and etiquette. Rules can be presented, *in Chinese*, on the first day and reviewed daily for the first week or so. The rules should be posted *in Chinese* in every classroom, with pictures to help clarify meaning. Experts in classroom management usually recommend that there be no more than five rules, focusing on the most important behaviors, and that they be worded simply and positively. An example of five common rules with pictures is found in the appendix. Five simple rules commonly used are:

1. Keep your eyes on the teacher 看老师
2. Listen 听
3. Raise your hand 举手
4. Keep your hands to yourself 把手放好
5. Speak Chinese 说中文

At the same time the rules are presented, teachers often present a "silent signal," that is, a signal from the teacher that all students should stop talking and pay attention to the teacher. Some teachers raise their hand above their head when they want attention, and each student who sees the raised hand stops talking and raises her/his own hand and shows the raised hand to classmates. Thus children share responsibility for quieting the classroom.

Jessica Haxhi, a Japanese teacher in Waterbury, CT, places her hands on her head, with elbows to the side, and students stop talking when they see the signal and place their own hands on their heads. Some teachers switch off the lights in the classroom when they want to quiet the students, although flicking lights on and off repeatedly can be distracting to some students and should be avoided.

The following strategies are based on those developed by Haxhi. They are suggested for teaching the rules *in Chinese*:

a. Introduce phrases using TPR gestures. For example, "look at the teacher" (看老师 touch fingers beside eyes and move them out to point to the teacher); "listen" (听— hands behind ears); "raise your hand" (请举手 — raising hand), "touch" (碰 — touching a student on the shoulder or hand), and "don't touch" (不要碰 — crossing arms across chest). "Speak English" (turn to a child and say "how are you? Hi! It's good to see you," etc. and have them turn to each other and do the same) "Speak Chinese." (说中文 Turn to class and greet them in Chinese, say anything else they know how to say in Chinese, and have them turn to each other and do the same.) Repeat many times with students.

b. After reviewing all of the expressions from the beginning many times and in different combinations, "test" by saying the words without showing the gestures. Then, tell students to close their eyes and perform the gestures that you command.

c. After this listening comprehension check, show students the word signs or posters for each expression as you say it. Encourage students to act out gestures. After some practice, stop saying the words and just silently show the signs to the students, having them "read" the expressions and perform the gestures (assessment).

d. It is also important to explain any other class management system you may be using, such as a stamp or star chart for daily following of the rules, etc.

e. Review the class rules daily for the first week or two of school and as necessary. Consistently use the same class rules during class management throughout the year, coupled with gestures and pointing to the class rules posted in your room when needed.

Classroom Etiquette and Commands

Like the rules, routines must be modeled and taught, usually one at a time. For example, an opening routine of bowing to the teacher and greeting the teacher will be learned quickly, without the focused teaching needed for the rules.

Some directions and procedures can be taught effectively through the use of TPR, usually as they are needed to manage class activities. As described in the TPR discussion in the Introduction, teachers begin by modeling the response to the command, then removing the model to test comprehension, and then changing the order of the commands. Some of the most common of these classroom commands include the following:

站起来 /起立	Stand up
坐下	Sit down
请手	Raise your hand
把手放下	Put down your hand
把书打开	Open the book
把书关起来	Close the book

把铅笔拿出来	Take out the pencil
把铅笔放下	Put down the pencil
来排成一行	line up
排队	line up into a team
围成一圈	form a circle
慢慢走	Walk — slowly — quietly
摸	Touch—your *eyes, ears, nose, mouth, knees, head, feet, arms, shoulders, elbows*

The teacher may wish to post these commands with pictures to remind students of their meaning. In most cases, however, the modeling by the teacher will be sufficient to help students recall the meaning of the command.

Classroom as a Print-Rich Environment

Even though young learners will not actually be reading Chinese for some time, the presence of meaningful written Chinese in the classroom is an important step in Chinese literacy. We encourage teachers to label the objects in the classroom with their Chinese names, and to post classroom rules, passwords, and language ladders. The icons below and the words associated with them may also be posted, as they are needed. The print in the classroom, together with the print in the student book and the workbook, will serve as a rich resource for students as they grow in their ability to associate the hanzi with meanings.

This table contains a list of instruction words associated with common classroom activities. They can be introduced in context, as needed, and then posted around the classroom for student reference.

Useful Icons for Class Management and Workbook

Icon	Instruction	Icon	Instruction
A picture of an eye	看一看 Look	A picture of a pencil and paper	写一写 Write
A picture of a mouth	说一说 Say or speak	A picture of scissors	剪一剪 Cut
A picture of an ear	听一听 Listen	A picture of Glue	贴一贴 Paste
A picture of a book	读一读 Read	A picture of a crayon	画一画 Draw
Show a pen making a circle	圈一圈 Circle	A magnifying glass	找一找 Find/Look for
An arrow	连一连 Match	A picture of a paint brush	涂颜色 Color

DESIGNING THE DAILY LESSON PLAN

Each lesson in the student book and workbook is intended to provide materials for one week of classes that meet daily for 30 minutes. Each class session should allow for both recycling of previously learned language and introduction and practice of new language, using a great variety of activities: songs, chants, fingerplays (in grades PK-1), rhymes, short conversations, TPR (see introduction), partner activities, stories, culturally-based crafts, and other age-appropriate activities. Puppets, stuffed animals, and visuals of all kinds will enhance the lesson and encourage learners to participate. When planning the daily lesson, the teacher should keep in mind the importance of changing activities frequently, and of alternating high-energy activities with less intensive activities. Children in PK-1 learn best when they are not expected to sit still for more than a few minutes at a time.

Brain research tells us that the first and last five minutes of a class period are *prime learning time* for our students, the best time for learning new material and making it memorable. At the same time, regular opening and closing routines are valuable for managing the classroom, making children comfortable, and giving essential practice. For this reason the lesson template below limits the amount of time for opening and closing routines, and places the introduction of new material early in the lesson.

DAILY LESSON TEMPLATE

Objectives

By the end of this lesson, students will be able to:

Include targeted standards at the end of each objective (1.1, 2.2, etc.).

Materials needed

Lesson Outline

• Opening routine: song, chant, greetings (2 min.)

• Preview, review, and "teaser": (3 min.)

>   Use TPR sequence, an interactive activity, and/or interesting props to spark student curiosity and introduce new language from the coming lesson.

>   Use visuals, props, and gestures in a quick, interactive review of material necessary for the new lesson.

• The "Big Event":

>   Extended listening experience, supported by props and visuals (5 min.):

>   Use story, explanation, demonstration, song, rhyme, etc. to introduce new language or recombine language from several lessons.

>   Building on previously learned language, use an activity such as a game, song, chant, fingerplay, or partner activity to practice new material. (10 min.)

• Tone practice (game-like activity) (2 min.)

• Literacy activity (3 min.)
     Hanzi acquisition
     Sight vocabulary development

• Quick wrap-up/review (3 min.)

• Closing routine: song, chant, greetings (2 min.)

Formative Assessment and Record Keeping

Identify which parts of the lesson could be used for formative assessment, or for recording student performance.

Beyond the Classroom

What activities might the students take home to share? What might they do outside of class to build their skills?

Reflection

What went well? What needs more work in the next lesson? Which students need special attention next time? What activities shall I do differently?

Routines play an important role in the Chinese class. Opening routines help to prepare the students for the class and the new language, and closing routines prepare students for the transition to their next class. They also give children experiences with culturally appropriate gestures and phrases. Routines for transitions help to transfer some of the responsibility for classroom management to the students themselves.

1. Beginning
   a. Greeting:
   Using Total Physical Response (TPR), teacher says: 起立。(Stand up).
   Teacher then says, "鞠躬" or "敬礼"(Bow) and demonstrates to students to how to bow.
   Teacher teaches the students to say: "老师好" (Hello, Teacher) and teacher responds by saying
   "小朋友好" (Hello, little friends).

   After students bow to the teacher, the class remains standing and teacher signals the class to sing the song, "你好" (How Are You). Using the tune of London Bridge Is Falling Down, sing this song:

   你好，你好，你好吗？我很好，谢谢你。

   你好，你好，你好吗？我很好，谢谢你。

   Students bow to one another. Then Teacher says: 坐下 (Sit down) and signals students to sit down.

   b. 今天天气怎么样？ (**How's the Weather Today?**)
   We suggest a weather component in the opening routine, using some kind of visual that has several types of weather pictured. A weather wheel is useful, as is a weather chart. One good approach is to create a graph, including the various types of weather being taught (sunny, cloudy, rain, snow, for example) and hang interlocking rings under the appropriate type of weather each day. This results in a graph of weather over a period of time. It also gives introduction and review of weather concepts, including hot and cold.

Procedures: Teacher brings out the weather chart and goes to the window, asking "What is the weather like today?" Using the chart, the teacher points to the appropriate weather symbol, i.e., (Pointing to sun symbol) "Ooo-it's sunny. Is it hot (mopping brow)? Is it cold? (hugging arms together and shivering). After several days, perhaps with different weather, the teacher might call a child forward, using the phrase and gesture "come here, please," and send the child to the window (or the door) and then ask "Is it sunny? Is it raining? etc. and then follow up with "Is it hot? No, it is not hot, it is cold. (Or whatever it is appropriate—starting with the opposite of the actual weather or temperature.) When students show understanding of the weather terms and temperatures, Teacher tells them "Tell your partner, 'It is sunny (cold, cloudy, hot, windy, etc.)'" The child who went to the window or door can hang a ring under the appropriate picture.

2. Transitional Routines

When it is time to move from one activity or one part of the classroom to another, teachers can use a number of routines to help alert students to the change. Some teachers use a rhythmic clapping pattern that the students join as soon as they hear it. Other teachers have a song to indicate a change of activity, for example from seatwork to group work: "Put it away, put it away, put everything away, put it away, put it away, put it away now." Or another example, "Come to the circle, come to the circle, come to the circle now."

3. Tone Exercise Routines

On each page in each lesson, there will be Chinese characters (hanzi) that use the same tone listed on the bottom of the page. There will also be a Tone Policeman with his arm stretched to indicate the pitch of the tone. Teachers should make it a routine exercise to practice tones for a few minutes every day. Using TPR, teachers say sounds with the designated tones and demonstrate the arm position for the tone(s) being practiced. They then ask students to act as the Tone Police, using their arms to indicate the specific tone they hear. When the teacher feels that students have good control of the tone, the Teacher can ask a student to say the tone while the rest of the class acts like the tone Police.

4. Literacy Practice Routine

See the strategies above. Teacher may decide to do this at a certain point during the opening class routine.

5. End of Class Routine

On each day at the end of the class, laoshi leads the whole class in reciting and acting out the text studied for the day. On the last day of the lesson, laoshi may use the I can statements as guideposts for wrapping up. Then the following procedures are suggested in order to bring the daily lesson to an end:

Using Total Physical Response (TPR), teacher says: 起立。(Stand up).

The teacher will signal the class to sing the Good-bye song, "再见歌".

Using the tune of a Chinese song called, 欢迎，谢谢，再见 (Welcome, Thank you, Good-bye) sing this song:

> 谢谢, 谢谢,
> 谢谢老师。
> 再见，再见，
> 大家再见，
> 再见，再见，再见!

Teacher then says "鞠躬" or "敬礼" (Bow) and demonstrates to students how to bow. Teacher teaches the students to say: "谢谢老师。老师再见"（Thank you, Teacher. Good-bye, Teacher）and Teacher will respond by saying "小朋友再见"（Little friends, Good-Bye）.

KINDERGARTEN : MY FRIEND PINGPING
我的朋友平平

To be updated

KA: Sun Wukong Comes to Visit Me
孙悟空来看我

L	Main Content	I Can Statements (for students): I can	Language Functions (for teachers)	Major activities (TG & WB)
1	**P.1** (莉莉)妈妈，你看，这是什么? *(Mommy, look! What is this?)* **P.2** (妈妈)啊，好奇怪的石头! *(Ah! What a strange rock!)* **P.3** (莉莉)妈妈，我可以带它回家吗? *(Mommy, may I take it home?)* (妈妈)可以。 *(Sure.)* **P.4** (莉莉)石头、石头，陪我睡觉…… *(Rock, rock, sleep with me....)* P.5 我会认: 石	1. ask what something is 2. ask for permission **Literacy Development:** recognize the *hanzi* "石", know what it means and how to pronounce it	1. asking and giving permission 2. asking for information **Literacy:** match the printed shape, sound, and meaning of a Chinese character (*hanzi*)	• Magic bag, use classroom objects also • Guessing game with "What is this?" • Use strange pencil, strange crayon, etc. Introduce passwords with "May I" go to the bathroom. • Rock and chant the song

Worksheet

43

- Have class close their eyes (TPR)
- Make something disappear—finding game
- Model "who are you" with puppets first, then ask children to tell who they are, using wo shi (name).

1. asking for information (where)
2. asking for information (who)

Literacy:
match the printed shape, sound, and meaning of a Chinese character (hanzi)

1. ask where something is
2. ask who someone is
3. sing the song "石头在哪里" with the class

Literacy Development:
recognize the hanzi "小", know what it means and how to pronounce it

2

P.6
(莉莉)妈妈，石头不见了！
(Mommy, the rock disappeared!)

P.7
(莉莉)石头在哪里？
(Where's the rock?)

P.8
(莉莉)石头在哪里？
(Where's the rock?)

P.9
(妈妈)唉，哪里来的小猴子？
(Oh, my! Where did this little monkey come from?)

P.10
(莉莉)小猴子，你是谁啊？
(Little Monkey, who are you?)

P.11
(我会唱)
石头在哪里？
石头，石头，
在哪里？在哪里？
石头你在哪里？
石头你在哪里？
不见了，不见了！

3	P.12 我会认认小 P.13 (莉莉)小猴子，你是谁啊？ *(Little Monkey, who are you?)* (孙悟空)我是孙悟空！ *(I am Sun Wukong!)* P.14 (莉莉)你从哪里来的？ *(Where did you come from?)* P.15 (孙悟空)我是你带回来的！ *(I was brought back by you!)* (莉莉)是吗？ *(Really?)* P.16 (孙悟空)我是那块石头变的！我从中国来。 *(I changed from that rock! I came from China.)* (莉莉)哦，太好了！ *(Oh, that's great!)*	1. tell who am 2. ask where someone comes from 3. locate China on the globe or map 4. use "是吗？" to show I understand and am surprised 5. suggest to someone that we be friends 6. agree with someone **Literacy Development:** recognize the *hanzi* "中", know what it means and how to pronounce it	1. Identifying oneself 2. Asking where someone comes from 3. Identifying location (China) on a map or globe 4. Inviting friendship 5. Expressing agreement **Literacy:** match the printed shape, sound, and meaning of a Chinese character (*hanzi*)	• Finding China on map, globe • Matching name for China on the map. *at home* • Locate China on the map or on the globe • Read children's book "The Making of Monkey King" • Show video of "Monkey King" • Dialog: Where are you from? Where is China?

			Games: 1. copycat 2. Please follow me（请你这样跟我做） Gouin series
		1. Narrating personal experiences 2. Expressing shared experience (ye) **Literacy:** match the printed shape, sound, and meaning of a Chinese character (*hanzi*)	
4	P.17 (莉莉)我是莉莉。我们交个朋友吧! *(I'm Lily. Let's make a friend with each other!)* (孙悟空)好啊! *(Okay!)* P.18 我会认: 中 P.19 (莉莉)我刷牙。 *(I brush my teeth.)* (孙悟空)我也刷牙。 *(I brush my teeth, too.)* P.20 (莉莉)我洗脸。 *(I wash my face.)* (孙悟空)我也洗脸。 *(I wash my face, too.)* P.21 (莉莉)我梳头。 *(I comb my hair.)* (孙悟空)我也梳头。 *(I comb my hair, too.)*	1. follow the teacher's instructions to act out the daily routines 2. tell and act out a morning routine 3. say that I can do something, too 4. sing and act out the song "我们这样来刷牙" with the class **Literacy Development:** recognize the *hanzi* "衣", know what it means and how to pronounce it	

		• TPR: jump, dance, walk • Introducing to each other
		1. Greeting (polite and informal) and thanking 2. Introducing
	1. greet and thank friends and my teacher 2. introduce someone	
5	P.26–27 (莉莉)老师好!同学们好! (*Hello, Teacher. Hello, classmates.*) P.22 (莉莉)我穿衣服。 (*I get dressed.*) (孙悟空)我也穿衣服。 (*I get dressed, too.*) P.23 (莉莉)我背书包。 (*I carry my backpack.*) (孙悟空)我也背书包。 (*I carry my backpack, too.*) P.24 (我会唱)我们这样来刷牙 我们这样来刷牙，来刷牙，来刷牙;我们这样来刷牙，每天的早上。 (*This is the way I brush my teeth, brush my teeth, brush my teeth. This is the way I brush my teeth, early in the morning*) P.25 我会认: 衣		

47

	Literacy Development: recognize the hanzi "人", know what it means and how to pronounce it	Literacy: match the printed shape, sound, and meaning of a Chinese character (*hanzi*)	• Introducing a new puppet • Introducing selves • Practicing polite forms "您"
P.26–27 (莉莉)老师好！同学们好！ (*Hello, Teacher. Hello, classmates.*) (孙悟空)啊，这里好多人呀！ (*Wow, there's so many people here!*) **P. 28** (老师)莉莉，你好吗？ (*Lily, How are you?*) (莉莉)我很好，谢谢您。 (*I'm fine. Thank you.*) **P.29** (莉莉)这是我的新朋友，他叫孙悟空。 (*This is my new friend. His name is Sun Wukong.*) (孙悟空)老师您您好！大家好！ (*Hello, teacher! Hello, everyone!*) (大家)孙悟空，你好！ (*Hello, Sun Wukong!*) **P.30** 我会认：人			

| 6 | P.31
(大永)孙悟空，你会做什么？
(Sun Wukong, What can you do?)

(孙悟空)我什么都会。
(I can do everything.)

p.32
(荷西)我会画画。
(I can draw.)
(孙悟空)我也会画画。
(I can draw, too.)

P.33
(爱子)我会唱歌。
(I can sing.)
(孙悟空)我也会唱歌。
(I can sing, too.)

P.34
(珍妮)我会跳舞。
(I can dance.)
(孙悟空)我也会跳舞。
(I can dance, too.) | 1. ask someone what they can do
2. ask and tell what else they can do
3. boast about something I can do
4. sing the song "一个拇指动一动" with the class

Literacy Development:
recognize the hanzi "大", know what it means and how to pronounce it | 1. Asking for information
2. boasting
3. expressing shared experience (ye)
4. expressing change

Literacy:
match the printed shape, sound, and meaning of a Chinese character (*hanzi*) | • practice with big and small doing character writing
• game: charade |

		Literacy Development: recognize the hanzi "人", know what it means and how to pronounce it	Literacy: match the printed shape, sound, and meaning of a Chinese character (*hanzi*)	• Introducing a new puppet • Introducing selves • Practicing polite forms "您"
7	P.35 (荷西)孙悟空，你还会什么？ (*Sunwukong, what else can you do?*) (孙悟空)我还会变大和变小! (*I can make myself bigger and smaller!*) P.36 (荷西)哈哈，莉莉，你的新朋友真好玩! (*Haha, Lily, your new friend is so much fun!*) P.37 (我会唱)一个拇指动一动 一个拇指动一动， 一个拇指动一动。 大家唱唱歌， 大家跳跳舞， 真快乐! P.38　我会认：大 P.39 (老师)大家吃点心了! (*It's time for your snack!*) P. 40 (莉莉)我好饿。 (*I am hungry.*)		1. tell others it is time to do something new 2. tell someone that I'm hungry 3. tell someone I need to go to the bathroom and wash my hands	1. announcing a change of activity 2. expressing hunger 3. stating necessity and need	• Passwords • Gouin series

Literacy Development:
recognize the *hanzi* "手", know what it means and how to pronounce it

Literacy:
match the printed shape, sound, and meaning of a Chinese character (*hanzi*)

(孙悟空)我也好饿。
(*I am hungry, too.*)

P. 41
(大永)我要上厕所。
(*I want to go to the bathroom.*)

(孙悟空)我也要上厕所。
(*I want to go to the bathroom, too.*)

P. 42
(爱子)我要洗手。
(*I want to wash my hands.*)

(孙悟空)我也要洗手。
(*I want to wash my hands, too.*)

p. 43
我会认：手

1. offer something to eat or drink
2. ask what's wrong
3. say that I want to go home
4. show that I feel sorry for someone
5. show I am surprised with words

1. Offering food and drink
2. Rejecting an offer
3. Inquiring about health
4. Stating necessity and need
5. Expressing surprise (ai ya)

It's time to ...
• go home.
• go back to class.
• sleep.
• wash your hands.
• brush teeth.
• wash your face.
• comb your hair.
• get dressed.
• eat snacks.

8

P.44
(莉莉)孙悟空，你要喝水吗？
(*Sun Wukong, do you want water?*)
(孙悟空)不要。
(*No.*)

- drink water.
- go back to China.

Literacy: match the printed shape, sound, and meaning of a Chinese character (*hanzi*)

6. sing the song "小猴子" with the class

Literacy Development: recognize the hanzi "水", know what it means and

P. 45
(大永)你要吃饼干吗?
(Do you want cookies?)
(孙悟空)不要。
(No.)

P. 46
(荷西)你要吃苹果吗?
(Do you want an apple?)
(孙悟空)不要。
(No.)

P. 47
(爱子)你要吃香蕉吗?
(Do you want a banana?)
(孙悟空)不要。
(No.)

P. 48
(莉莉)哎呀，你怎么了? 你生病了吗?
(What's the matter? Are you sick?)
(孙悟空)没有。
(No.)

P. 49
(孙悟空)我要回家，我要回中国。
(I want to go home. I want to go back to China.)

P. 50 (我会唱小猴子) 小猴子，吱吱叫， 肚子饿了不能跳， 给香蕉，它不要， 你说好笑不好笑？ **P. 51** 我会认：水			
9	**P.52–53** (大永)孙悟空，你下来吧。 *Sun Wukong, come down.* (荷西)我们一起画画。 *Next time we'll draw together.* (爱子)我们一起唱歌。 *Next time we'll sing together.* (珍妮)我们一起跳舞。 *Next time we'll dance together.* **P.54** (孙悟空)不，我不下来。我要飞到天上去，我要飞到中国去。 *(No, I will not going down. I want to fly into the sky, and fly back to China.)*	1. ask someone/something to come down; 2. tell things I want to do with my friends 3. explain what Sun Wukong wants to do 4. tell someone goodbye and welcome back **Literacy Development:** recognize the *hanzi* "上" and "下", know what it means and how to pronounce it	1. Making a request 2. Stating needs and wants 3. Making promises for activities 4. Rejecting offers 5. Saying goodbye **Literacy:** match the printed shape, sound, and meaning of a Chinese character (*hanzi*)	• Come down 下来 • Tian shang 天上 (up in the sky) • Origami: Make a paper airplant. Students will fly the airplane and use the language fly up and fly down.

P.55 孙悟空再见！欢迎你再来玩！ *(Sun Wukong, good-bye! Come to visit us again!)* P.56 我会认: 上、下 P.57 "I Can" Statements		
大家一起来！（评估） *(Performance Assessment Tasks)*	10	
	PT	

*L : Lesson
PT: Performance Task

Classroom Rules

 Look at the Laoshi 看老师

 Listen 听

 Raise your hand 举手

 Keep hands to yourself 把手放好

 Speak Chinese 说中文

Rubrics for interpretive task

Student responds appropriately when asked to perform:

Task	Yes	With Help	Not Yet
Item 1			
Item 2			
Item 3			
Item 4			

Holistic Assessment Interpretive Task	Exceeds Expectations	Meets Expectations	Does Not Meet Expectations
Overall Performance			
Laoshi Comments			

Rubrics for interpersonal task

Student participates in brief conversation appropriately using memorized language:

Task	Yes, with some personalizing	Yes, using only memorized language	Yes, with prompting or some mistakes
Item 1			
Item 2			
Item 3			
Item 4			

Student participates in brief conversation appropriately using memorized language:

Task	Yes, with almost no problems	Required some prompting or correcting to clarify meaning	Partial participation only, with much prompting
Item 1			
Item 2			
Item 3			
Item 4			

Holistic Assessment Interpersonal Task	Exceeds Expectations	Meets Expectations	Does Not Meet Expectations
Overall Performance			
Laoshi Comments			

Rubrics for presentational task

Student presents or participates in presentation of memorized chunks in songs, rhymes, or other tasks:

Task	Yes, with original recombinations	Yes, using only memorized language	Yes, with prompting or some mistakes
Item 1			
Item 2			
Item 3			
Item 4			

Student pronunciation and grammar are understandable by Laoshi and fellow students:

Task	Yes, with few problems	Requires prompting and correcting to clarify meaning	Partial participation only, with much prompting
Item 1			
Item 2			
Item 3			
Item 4			

Holistic Assessment Presentational Task	Exceeds Expectations	Meets Expectations	Does Not Meet Expectations
Overall Performance Laoshi Comments			

Rubrics for literacy task

Student can name, trace and identify _____. (Strokes, stroke orders, character components, characters, as appropriate)

Task	Yes, consistently without errors	Yes, with prompting or with minor errors	Not Yet
Item 1			
Item 2			
Item 3			
Item 4			

Student can recognize, read, or write characters, phrases, or sentences, as appropriate:

Task	Yes, consistently without errors	Yes, with prompting or with minor errors	Not Yet
Item 1			
Item 2			
Item 3			
Item 4			

Holistic Assessment Literacy Task	Exceeds Expectations	Meets Expectations	Does Not Meet Expectations
Overall Performance Laoshi Comments			

Holistic Summative Assessment

(alternative to or replacement for the above)

Task	Exceeds Expectations Consistent performance, some creativity and personal application evident.	Meets Expectations Consistent performance with learned and memorized materials	Does Not Meet Expectations Inconsistent and often incorrect performance. Does not complete the task.
Interpretive			
Interpersonal			
Presentational			
Literacy			
TonesLiteracy			
Laoshi Comments			

Dear parents and caregivers,

It is a pleasure to have your child learning Chinese in my class this year. As you may know, Chinese is spoken by more people throughout the world than any other language, including English. It has become increasingly important for Americans to learn the Chinese language and understand Chinese culture.

Children are at an ideal age to begin learning a new language, especially a language so different from their own. It takes many years to learn any new language well. An early start with Chinese will give learners the opportunity to develop useful language skills over a number of years. At the same time, they will enrich their understanding of the world and become more skillful with their native language.

If you come to visit our classroom, you will see that the lessons are presented in Chinese and without translation into English. It is natural for children to learn first through listening and responding. As they become more confident with the language they will begin to speak more Chinese all the time, and the songs, rhymes, and chants they learn in class will probably also become very familiar at home! Because written Chinese is so different from written English, it will be introduced very slowly, one character at a time.

Even though you may not speak Chinese yourself, there are some things you can do at home to help your child learn this new language. Show interest in the Chinese classes and enthusiasm for the fact that your child is learning Chinese. Invite your child to show what has been learned, but please do not ask for a translation into English or into Chinese. Since that is not a part of what we teach (translation is a very advanced skill), your child may be frustrated and feel unsuccessful. I will regularly send home lists of "I can" statements, so that you can know what is realistic to expect from your child. If the "I can" statement is: "I can greet someone in Chinese," you might ask your child, "How do you greet someone in Chinese?"

Another way to help your child is to seek out experiences related to the Chinese language and culture. Chinese musicians and acrobats tour the country from time to time, and there are sometimes TV specials that relate to Chinese arts and culture. There is a growing number of picture books and story books drawn from Chinese culture or illustrated by Chinese artists. From time to time I may send home suggestions for Chinese Web sites or videos, and I invite you to let me know about your discoveries, so they can be shared with other families.

Right now we are beginning work on a unit called:
The focus of this unit is:
and the children will be learning about:
They will be learning to use Chinese to:

If you have questions or concerns about our Chinese program, please feel free to contact me at:
I look forward to our work together with the Chinese language and culture.

Suggested Passwords for *Flying with Chinese*

May I please…	我可以……
go to the bathroom?	上厕所吗？
sharpen my pencil?	削铅笔吗？
go to my locker?	去开柜子吗？
get a drink of water?	去喝水吗？
go to the office?	去办公室吗？
borrow a pencil?	借一支铅笔吗？
have a tissue?	拿一张纸巾吗？
I don't know.	我不知道。
I don't understand.	我不明白。
Would you repeat that please?	请再说一遍，好吗？
Would you speak more slowly, please?	请说得慢一些，好吗？
Can you help me?	请帮个忙，好吗？
How do you say ＿＿ in Chinese?	这个＿＿中文怎么说？
I can't find my eraser	我找不到橡皮了。
(paper, book, homework, lunch ticket, etc.)	（纸、书、作业本、午餐券）
May I borrow that?	我可以借你的＿＿吗？
(your pencil, your book, your eraser, etc.)	（铅笔、书、橡皮）
Please pass me the scissors (red/blue/yellow marker, paste, pencil, pen, etc.)	请把（剪刀、红／蓝／黄笔、胶水、铅笔、圆珠笔）递给我。
Please give me the jump rope (ball, key, book, etc.).	请给我（绳子、皮球、钥匙、书）。
I'll share that with you.	我们共用……
That is mine. (That belongs to me.)	这是我的。（那是我的。）
Show me…	给我看……
Sit down next to me.	坐在我旁边吧。
Do you know how to play?	你知道怎么玩吗？
I have a headache (stomach ache, sore throat/hand/foot/leg, etc.)	我头痛（肚子痛、喉咙痛、手痛、脚痛、腿痛）
Don't look at my paper.	别看我的作业。
He/She is sitting in my place.	他/她坐了我的位置。
Please leave me alone.	别烦我。

Vocabulary and Grammar

Radicals	三点水，草字头，木字旁，口字旁，提手旁，单人旁，金字旁（繁体），提土旁，虫字旁，竖心旁，金字旁（简体），月肉旁，女字旁，竹字头，绞丝旁（繁体），山字旁，石字旁，言字旁，斜玉旁，绞丝旁（简体）
Numbers	一，二，三，四，五，六，七，八，九，十，百，千，万
Pictographs	天地山林，水火土石，风雪云雨，日月星光，木术王玉，禾电田苗
Nature	海，河，湖，池塘，江，山，草原，森林，树木，叶，花，草，竹子，金
Animals	鼠牛虎兔，龙蛇马羊，猴鸡狗猪，鸟鱼虫猫，大象，狮子，属什么
Body Parts	人口头舌，牙耳目眉，心，脸，鼻，毛发，肩膀，膝盖，手指足脚，身体，嘴巴
Five Senses	酸甜苦辣，香臭，软硬，摸，闻，看，听，说，唱，吃，喝
Feelings and Emotions	哭，笑，高兴，喜欢，舒服，讨厌，麻烦，生病，吃药
Family	爷奶爸妈，叔姨伯姑，哥姐弟妹，儿子，女儿，孩子，孙子
People	男，女，老，幼，小孩，小朋友，友，老师，警察，大夫（医生），消防员，校长，护士，邮差，名字，姓名
Pronouns	你，我，它，她，他，……们，……的，自己
Colors	红，橙，黄，绿，青，蓝，紫，黑，白，颜色，彩色，彩虹，棕色
Seasons	春夏秋冬，暖热凉冷。冰冻，天气
Holidays	节，春节，元宵节，清明节，端午节，中秋节，重阳节，度假，寒假，暑假，请假，万圣节，圣诞节，新年，生日，快乐，庆祝，祝你，恭喜发财，万事如意，健康快乐
Cultural Terms	京剧。舞龙，舞狮。扯铃，中国结，面具。Others.
Food	米，饭，面，汤，菜，肉，豆腐，饺子，蛋，蛋糕，包子，馒头，面包。牛排，虾，海鲜，茶，咖啡，水果类，糖
Clothing	衣，帽，裤，鞋，袜，裙，厚，薄，外套，围巾，手套，眼镜，表

Sports	球，篮球，足球，棒球，网球，（操）场，乒乓球，溜冰，滑雪 投，丢，接 琴，棋，比赛……赛……
Building and Household	房子，门，窗，桌，椅，灯，扇，钟，碗，筷，刀，叉，盘，匙
Classroom & Common Objects	学校，教室，笔墨纸砚，琴棋书画，计算机，school subjects，卡片， 礼物，考试，课本，作业本，上网，电子邮件（电邮）
Leisure Activities	看，电影，电视，买东西，逛街，运动，跳舞，唱歌，戏
Transportation	车，船，飞机，走路
Math	加，减，乘，除
Time words	早，晚，点，中午，下午，小时，钟头，星期，月，年， 今天，明天，昨天，后天，前天，今年，明年，去年，后年 日历，现在，刚才，以后，以前，后来，然后，从前，时间， 有时候，通常，平常，常
Sizes	大，中，小
Position & Directions	上，下，左，右，高，低，远，近，前，后，里，外，东，西，南， 北，旁，边，上，下（来，去），起来
Shapes	方，圆，长，短，三角形，菱形，形状，粗，细，直，弯曲。
Adjectives	好，坏，胖，瘦，美，丑，轻，重，干净
Verbs	是，对，有
Verbs	玩，行，走，跑，跳，爬，滑，踏，蹲下来。坐，站立，站起来，追，赶，推，拉，拔，碰，躲，藏，找，抓，刷，洗，打，躺，睡，醒，休息，睡觉。听，说，读，写。想，唱。咬，喊，叫，吹，问，答，骂，吵，学，闹，画，喜欢，有没有，爱，要，来，去。开，关，剪，拿，搬，请，谢，对不起。进出，穿，带，戴，住，祝，卖，买，送
Adverbs	到，着，不，又，多，少，几，什么，为什么，出，来，快，慢，空，满，已经，还没有，还，或者，而且，……见（看见），只，才，就，常，平常
Measure Words	个，件，只，枝，本，张，条，双，片，群，把，间

Common Expressions	再见,…Other classroom and daily routine expressions
Basic Grammatical Structures	categorize by functions, to be entered by the team 因为……，所以……。 虽然……，可是（但是，不过）……。 …… …… …… …… …… ……

1. 他学习汉语。
2. 他努力学习汉语。
3. 他是中国人。
4. 他吃了饭。
5. 他去买东西。
6. 计算机公司。
7. 他有哥哥。
8. 他是知道。
9. 他昨天买了菜。
10. 打篮球。
11. 爸爸让我学汉语。
12. 爸爸让我每天看电视。
13. 我休息。
14. 他很忙。
15. 他没有哥哥。
16. 他喝咖啡还是喝茶?
17. 北京车是很多。
18. 我听懂了。
19. 爸爸忙。
20. 他住在上海。
21. 妈妈每天去买东西。
22. 现在我休息。
23. 打电话。
24. 他看着电视。
25. 他学了三年汉语。

These patterns appear more than 100 times, constituting 87% of the 25,000 hanzi being used in the database.

Junior Learner Profiles

	JR. NOVICE-LOW	JR. NOVICE-MID	JR. NOVICW-HIGH	JR. INTERMEDIATE-LOW	JR. INTERMEDIATE-MID	JR. INTERMEDIATE-HIGH
Comprehension Recognizes isolated words and high-frequency expressions.	Understands predictable questions, statements, and commands in familiar topic areas, supported by contextual clues, repetition at slower rate of speech.	Understands predictable questions, statements, and commands in familiar topic areas, and some new information supported by contextual clues, repetition, and rephrasing at slower rate of speech.	Understands new information and oral/ written messages in a limited number of areas with contextual support. Follows conversation at a fairly normal rate of speech.	Understands information and messages in new contexts though some slow downs may be necessary. My show some difficulty on unfamiliar topics.	Understands speech at normal speed most of the time. Fewer comprehension problems. Understands longer stretches of connected discourse on a number of topics.
Functional Ability Produces isolated words and/or high-frequency expressions. Has no functional communicative ability.	Uses a limited number of words and phrases, and some longer memorized expressions within predictable topic areas. Makes attempts to create with the language, but is unsuccessful. May use native language. Often makes long pauses.	Uses high-frequency expressions and other memorized expressions With ease. Signs of originality and spontaneity begin to emerge. Makes attempts to create with language with more success., but it is unable to sustain speech.	Able to handle a limited number of every day social and academic interactions. Maintains simple conversations. creates with language, although in a restrictive and reactive manner.	May initiate talk without relying on questions and prompts. Shows evidence of spontaneity. Gives simple descriptions successfully. May attempt longer and complex sentences with few connectors.	Maintains conversations with increasing fluency. Uses language creatively to initiate and sustain talk. Connected discourse is beginning to emerge in descriptions and narratives.
Vocabulary Recognizes and uses words and expressions related to concrete objects and actions on familiar topics.	Uses specific words, high-frequency expressions, and other longer, memorized expressions in a limited number of topic areas. Frequent searches for words.	Uses vocabulary centering on basic objects, actions, places, and common kinship terms, adequate for minimally elaborating utterances in predictable topic areas.	Has sufficient vocabulary for making statements and asking questions to satisfy basic social and academic needs, but not for explaining or elaborating on them.	Has basic vocabulary for discussions of a personal nature and on limited topics. Gaps may exist for speaking about topics of general interest. Attempts circumlocution.	Has a broad enough vocabulary for discussing simple social and academic topics in generalities, but lacks detail. Achieves successful circumlocution.
Grammar Uses memorized chunks accurately, but lacks grammar awareness.	Uses memorized expressions accurately. Attempts at putting together two or three word phrases. Limited grammar awareness.	Relies on memorized expressions. Creates some sentence-level speech. Attempts to use verbs.	Goes beyond memorized utterances to create with the language. Uses verbs. Speech may contain many grammatical inaccuracies.	Maintains simple conversation, mostly in present tense although an awareness of other tenses may be evident. Many grammatical inaccuracies.	Uses present tense, but lacks control of the past tenses. Grammatical inaccuracies present.

Adapted from Center for Applied Linguistics Proficiency Exam and Student Oral Proficiency Assessment and the Delaware World Languages Performance Indicators (2004)